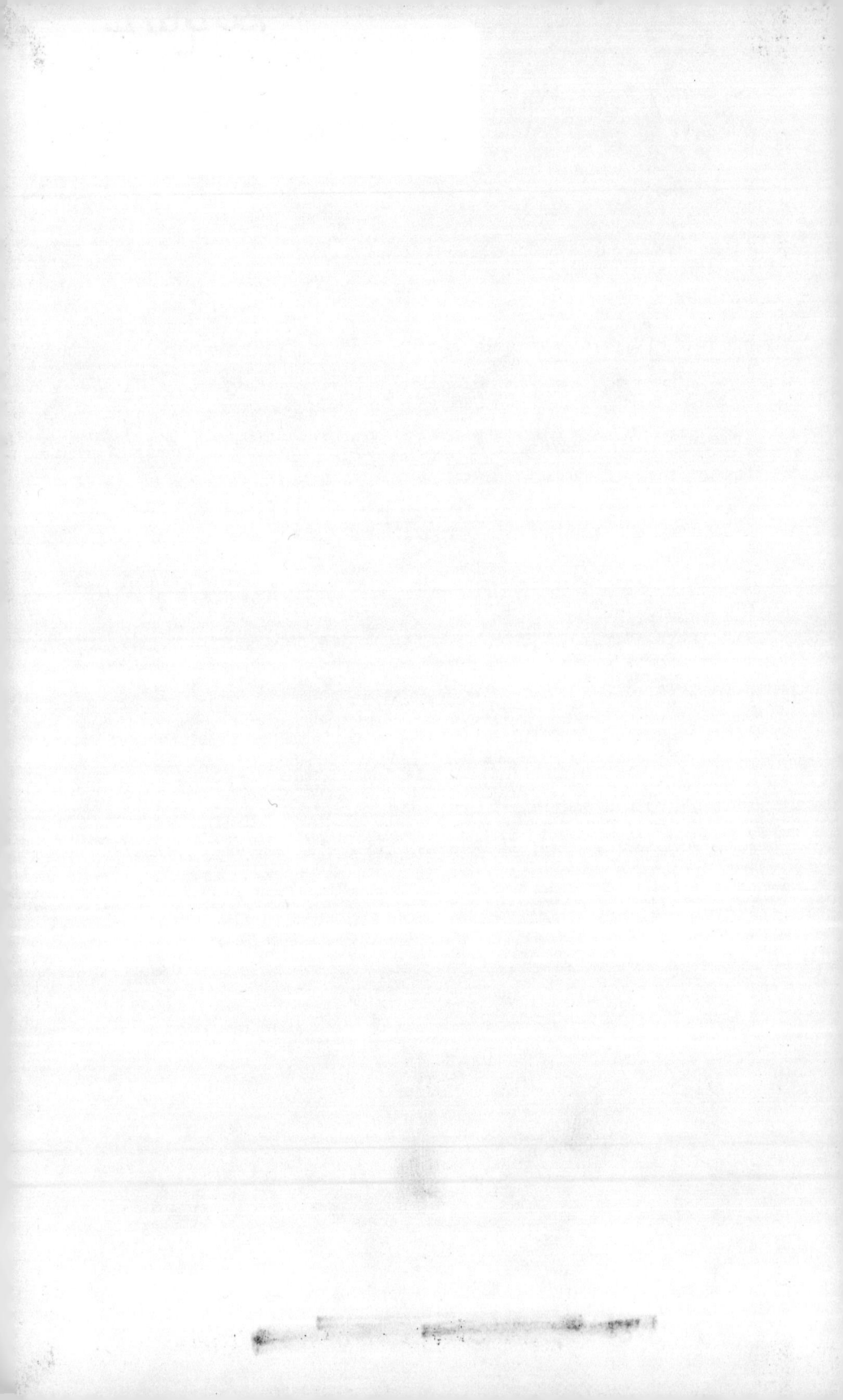

SPACE FLIGHT ADVENTURES AND DISASTERS

LIVING AND WORKING ABOARD THE INTERNATIONAL SPACE STATION

A MYREPORTLINKS.COM BOOK

HENRY M. HOLDEN

MyReportLinks.com Books

an imprint of

Enslow Publishers, Inc. E

Box 398, 40 Industrial Road
Berkeley Heights, NJ 07922
USA

MyReportLinks.com Books, an imprint of Enslow Publishers, Inc. MyReportLinks®
is a registered trademark of Enslow Publishers, Inc.

Library of Congress Cataloging-in-Publication Data

Holden, Henry M.
  Living and working aboard the International Space Station / Henry M.
Holden.
    p. cm. — (Space flight adventures and disasters)
Summary: Explains the construction and purpose of the International
Space Station and the life of the astronauts on board.
Includes bibliographical references and index.
  ISBN 0-7660-5168-4
  1. International Space Station—Juvenile literature. [1. International
Space Station.] I. Title. II. Series.
  TL797.15.H65 2004
  629.44'2—dc22
                        2003016486

Printed in the United States of America

10 9 8 7 6 5 4 3 2 1

To Our Readers:
Through the purchase of this book, you and your library gain access to the Report Links that specifically back
up this book.

The Publisher will provide access to the Report Links that back up this book and will keep these Report Links
up to date on **www.myreportlinks.com** for three years from the book's first publication date.

We have done our best to make sure all Internet addresses in this book were active and appropriate when we
went to press. However, the author and the Publisher have no control over, and assume no liability for, the
material available on those Internet sites or on other Web sites they may link to.

The usage of the MyReportLinks.com Books Web site is subject to the terms and conditions stated on the
Usage Policy Statement on **www.myreportlinks.com**.

A password may be required to access the Report Links that back up this book. The password is found on the
bottom of page 4 of this book.

Any comments or suggestions can be sent by e-mail to comments@myreportlinks.com or to the address on
the back cover.

Photo Credits: © 1995–2003 Public Broadcasting Service (PBS), p. 23; © 1999–2003 SPACE.com,
Inc., p. 11; © 2000 Discovery Communications, Inc., p. 40; © 2000–2003 European Space Agency,
p. 35; Kip Teague, NASA, p. 22; MyReportLinks.com, p. 4; National Aeronautics and Space
Administration (NASA), pp. 3, 9, 10, 12, 15, 16, 18, 20, 24, 26, 28, 31, 32, 36, 37, 38, 39, 42;
Photos.com, p. 1.

Cover Photo: NASA

Cover Description: A full view of the International Space Station.

Contents

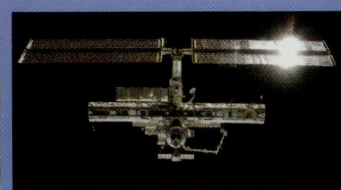

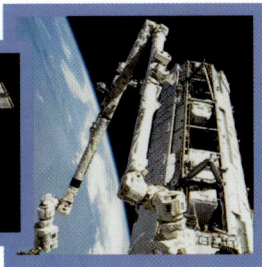

MyReportLinks.com Books
Great Books, Great Links, Great for Research!

The Report Links listed on the following four pages can save you hours of research time by **instantly** bringing you to the best Web sites relating to your report topic.

How to Use MyReportLinks.com

1 Got a Report to do?

2 Check out a MyReportLinks.com Book at the Library.

3 Read the Book.

4 Go to www.myreportlinks.com for Quick, Safe, and Up-to-Date Links!

5 Internet Report Links = Great Information.

6 Write Your Report. Impress Your Teacher.

MAX LYNX

The pre-evaluated Web sites are your links to source documents, photographs, illustrations, and maps. They also provide links to dozens—even hundreds—of Web sites about your report subject.

MyReportLinks.com Books and the MyReportLinks.com Web site save you time and make report writing easier than ever!

Please see "To Our Readers" on the copyright page for important information about this book, the MyReportLinks.com Web site, and the Report Links that back up this book. Please enter **FSS7009** if asked for a password.

Report Links

The Internet sites described below can be accessed at
http://www.myreportlinks.com

*Editor's Choice

▶**Space Station**

Explore the International Space Station. Learn what it is, its purpose,
and who the international partners are.

*Editor's Choice

▶**Inside the Space Station: Life in Space**

Discovery.com has a construction time line of the International Space
Station. Take interactive tours of the space station, and read about
its astronauts.

*Editor's Choice

▶**How Space Stations Work**

At the How Stuff Works Web site you can explore a variety of topics
related to space stations. These include how space stations work,
navigation, life support in space, and much more.

*Editor's Choice

▶**Space Junk: The Stuff Left Behind**

Learn about space junk—what it is, and how it got there. There is
also an image of the distribution of space junk around the earth.

*Editor's Choice

▶**International Space Station**

The Shuttle Presskit Online Web site profiles the International Space
Station. Topics covered include early assembly flights, assembly in orbit,
Russian missions, and much more.

*Editor's Choice

▶**Station Location**

Go to the Science@NASA Web site to see an image of where
the International Space Station is currently positioned.

Report Links

▶ After *Columbia*: The ISS in Crisis

When the space shuttle *Columbia* exploded, it slowed the progress of the ISS. This article from *Popular Science* magazine talks about the effects of the disaster.

▶ *Apollo-Soyuz* Test Project

At this Web site you will learn about the *Apollo-Soyuz* mission, the first human space flight mission involving two nations, the United States and Russia.

▶ Boeing: International Space Station

The Boeing Company was instrumental in creating the International Space Station. See about Boeing's role in the design, development, and testing of the International Space Station.

▶ Crew Return Vehicle (CRV)

Learn about the crew return vehicle (CRV) that will be in place at the International Space Station. This vehicle is an escape option designed to rescue crew members in space in the event of an emergency.

▶ Human Space Flight

At the Human Space Flight Web site you can read about space shuttles, the International Space Station, and other space related topics.

▶ International Space Station

Explore the International Space Station at NASA's Human Space Flight Web site. It will tell you about the space station crew, and let you view images from the space station.

▶ International Space Station: KSC

The Kennedy Space Center Web site features articles about the space station's location, hardware, and much more.

▶ ISS: The Main Elements

From the BBC News Web site you will learn about the main elements of the International Space Station, including the robotic arm and the functional cargo block.

Report Links

▶**Living in Space**
The NASA Human Space Flight Web site explores what it is like to live
in space, including what you would wear and what you would eat.

▶**Marshall Space Flight Center: History Office**
Read the biography of Dr. Wernher Von Braun on the Marshall Space Flight
Center Web site. Here you will learn about his initial conception of a space
station and his contributions to space exploration.

▶**NASA Quest**
The NASA Quest Web site gives online visitors an opportunity to explore
and learn about NASA. Here you can read the biographies of NASA
employees and learn about aerospace technology and space exploration events.

▶**National Aeronautic Space Administration**
At the official NASA Web site you have the opportunity to research a variety
of space-related topics, including missions, humans in space, and much more.

▶**Orbiting Junk Continues to Threaten International
Space Station**
Read this article discussing how "space junk" poses a threat to the International
Space Station.

▶**Personal Satellite Assistant**
The Ames Research Center Web site you will learn what a personal satellite
assistant is and how it works.

▶**Robonaut**
At this Web site you will learn about Robonaut, a humanoid. Described here
are different elements of Robonaut, including its hands, arms, and head control.

▶**Russia in Space: A Mini-History**
Read a brief history of the Russian space program from 1971 through 1986,
including the history of *Mir*.

Report Links

▶**See Learning in a Whole New Light**

The See Learning in a Whole New Light Web site describes what it is like to live in space, be an astronaut, and explore the galaxy.

▶*Skylab* **Kennedy Space Center**

Find out about *Skylab*, the United States' first manned space station, which was launched in 1973.

▶**Space-Age Living**

Learn about the International Space Station, including what it is, why it was built, where it is right now, and much more.

▶**Space Medicine**

Traveling in space can have some ill effects on the human body. Learn about how NASA is trying to prevent these ailments.

▶**Space Research Could Lower Gas Prices**

At the How Stuff Works Web site you can learn how space research could help lower gas prices.

▶**Space Station Assembly**

The NASA Human Space Flight Web site describes how the International Space Station is being assembled.

▶*Terror in Space*

PBS's *Terror in Space* series explores the history of the Soviet/Russian *Mir* space station and the complications it faced. The site also provides a virtual tour of *Mir*.

▶**What is Microgravity?**

This Web site provides a detailed definition of microgravity.

Any comments? Contact us: **comments@myreportlinks.com**

International Space Station Facts

Agreements to Create Station Signed	November 12, 1998
Launch Date of First Mission	October 31, 2000
Number of Flights Needed for Completion	45—Thirty-six Shuttle flights and nine Russian rocket launches were originally planned. This may change due to the Space Shuttle *Columbia* tragedy which caused NASA to ground all shuttle flights while it investigated the accident.
Weight at Completion	900,000 to 1 million pounds (408,233 to 453,000 kilograms)
Distance	The ISS orbits the Earth at an altitude of 240 miles (386 kilometers) above the Earth's surface.
Length	361 feet (about 110 meters)
Nations Participating	Sixteen—the United States; Russia; Canada; Belgium; Denmark; France; Germany; Italy; the Netherlands; Norway; Spain; Sweden; Switzerland; the United Kingdom; Japan; and Brazil.

Mission patch for Expedition 5 to the International Space Station. The names of the astronauts written on the sides of the patch are the crew members of the Space Shuttle. The top three names on the bottom were the astronauts going up to stay on the Space Station. The three names on the bottom were those returning to Earth.

Chapter 1

DANGER IN SPACE

It was Sunday, October 24, 1999. The U.S. Space Command, near Colorado Springs, was watching two objects on its radar. The objects, the International Space Station (ISS) and the remains of a Pegasus rocket, were screaming toward each other at a combined speed of almost 35,000 miles per hour (56,327 kilometers per hour). If they collided, the space station would be destroyed. The piece of rocket had been drifting in space for years, unable to return

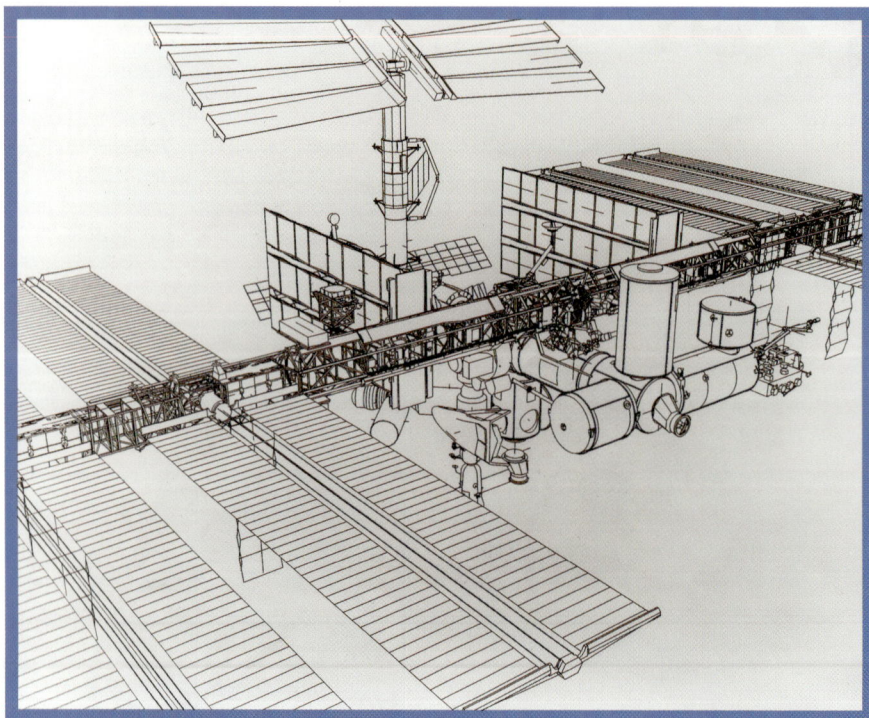

▲ *A line drawing of the original plans for the International Space Station. When it is completed, this is how it should look.*

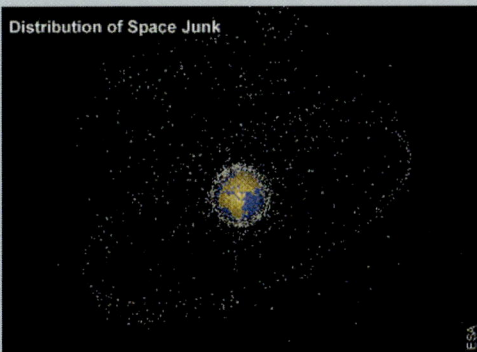

Distribution of Space Junk

The distribution of space junk around Earth.

▲ This image shows the location of the space junk that is currently orbiting Earth. Space junk presents a danger to the ISS and its crew.

to Earth. The ISS had only been in orbit about a year. Space Command predicted that the two would pass less than a mile apart. That was a serious threat to the ISS. Ground controllers remotely fired small engines on the ISS and changed its orbit slightly to prevent a possible collision with the old rocket.[1]

▶ Space Junk

The Space Command tracks about 8,900 objects, each at least the size of a baseball. More than six thousand are chunks of debris orbiting Earth.[2] This debris includes thousands of nuts, bolts, gloves, old satellites, and other

▲ *Astronauts David A. Wolf (left) and Piers J. Sellers (right) are performing a session of EVA. This stands for extravehicular activity, meaning that the astronauts are outside of the spacecraft.*

debris from space missions. It forms an orbiting garbage dump around Earth. More than two hundred objects, most of them trash bags, were released by the *Mir* space station.[3] The *Mir* station had been Russia's first space station. No one knows how much debris is out there. At least one piece destroyed a satellite. In 1996, a French satellite collided with a fragment of a rocket that had exploded in space ten years earlier. The impact sent the satellite spinning out of control.[4]

There are other objects, too small to be tracked from Earth, speeding through space. Small flecks of paint can damage a cockpit window on a space shuttle. For example, a tiny speck of paint from a satellite dug a pit in a space shuttle window almost a quarter-inch (.64 centimeters) wide.[5] "We get hit regularly on the shuttle," said Joseph Loftus, a NASA engineer. "We've replaced more than eighty [shuttle] windows because of debris impacts."[6]

One study estimated that there is about 4 million pounds of space junk in low-Earth orbit and about 110,000 objects larger than one centimeter, large enough to damage a satellite.[7] Fortunately, much of this debris will eventually burn up, falling back to Earth.

The ISS can be a dangerous place to work. Dust-sized meteorites can be a risk to space-walking astronauts. The particles whiz by at 17,500 miles per hour (28,163.5 kilometers per hour). These tiny objects are traveling faster than a bullet. To protect themselves, astronauts wear space suits that act like bullet-proof clothing. The suits are made of layers of Kevlar, Teflon, and aluminum Mylar. However, any hole or tear in the space suit could cause a rapid and fatal decompression. The risk to the astronauts is low because they are such small objects in space. Still, to lower the risk, they do not stay outside the ISS for long periods.

The ISS has not yet been damaged by space junk. Even so, NASA takes the risk seriously. Its scientists are reinforcing the station's most vulnerable parts during construction.

Chapter 2

BUILDING THE INTERNATIONAL SPACE STATION

Human space flight began in 1961. At first, the flights were short, but as humans learned more about space, the flights grew longer. In November 2003, the ISS marked a milestone in space history. Humans lived continuously in orbit for three years.

The International Space Station is the most ambitious engineering project in history, and the largest spacecraft ever put in orbit. The United States, United Kingdom, Russia, France, Germany, Italy, the Netherlands, Canada, Japan, Belgium, Norway, Denmark, Brazil, Sweden, Switzerland, and Spain are all helping by either supplying parts or astronauts. When finished, the station's internal volume will be about the size of two 747-jet passenger compartments.[1] The ISS will provide pressurized living and working space for a crew of up to seven.

▶ Construction

Parts for the ISS are carried in the cargo bay of the space shuttles. It will take about 160 spacewalks to assemble the ISS. When finished, it will be 361 feet (110 meters) wide, 290 feet (88 meters) long, about 14 stories high, and will weigh about 500 tons (about 1 million pounds).[2]

The ISS has three main sections. They are research modules, service modules, and living or habitation modules. Russia launched the first section of the ISS, the Zarya module, in November 1998. It provided the initial power and propulsion. The United States space shuttle *Endeavour*

▲ On November 20, 1998, the first portion of the ISS called the Zarya was launched into orbit from Kazakhstan.

ISS Expedition One Crew - Microsoft Internet Explorer

File   Edit   View   Favorites   Tools   Help

Address http://spaceflight.nasa.gov/station/crew/exp1/index.html

Mission Patch

ГИДЗЕНКО КРИКАЛЁВ
SHEPHERD

Mission Overview

Vehicle:	Russian Soyuz Rocket International Space Station Flight 2R
Launch Pad:	Baikonur Cosmodrome, Kazakhstan
Launch:	Oct. 31, 2000
Docking:	Nov. 2, 2000
Undocking:	March 18, 2001 STS-102
Increment Duration:	136 days, 17 hours, 9 minutes

From the left are Flight Engineer Sergei Krikalev, Expedition One Commander Bill Shepherd and Soyuz Commander Yuri Gidzenko.

ISS Commander	William M. (Bill) Shepherd	Crew Interview	Crew Menu
Soyuz Commander	Yuri Pavolich Gidzenko Rosaviakosmos	Crew Interview	Crew Menu
Flight Engineer	Sergei K. Krikalev Rosaviakosmos	Crew Interview	Crew Menu

* Expedition Three Crew served as a backup for this crew.

▲ *Expedition One was the first crew to live and work aboard the ISS. The crew, from left, was Flight Engineer Sergei Krikalev, Commander Bill Shepherd, and Commander Yuri Gidzenko.*

carried the U.S.-built 12-ton (26,880 pounds, 12,193 kilograms) Unity connecting module about two weeks later. These two modules had never been connected and had to fit perfectly the first time. *Endeavour*'s crew successfully attached the modules during the twelve-day mission.[3] A third section, Zvezda, joined up with the station in July 2000. Zvezda provided living quarters and life support systems. Destiny, the United States science laboratory, was attached in February 2001.

Expedition One

On October 31, 2000, astronaut William Shepherd and cosmonauts Yuri Gidzenko and Sergei Krikalev flew to the station on a Russian *Soyuz* rocket. They became the ISS's first full-time crew. Krikalev served as the flight engineer, responsible for the systems. Shepherd served as the expedition commander, and Gidzenko served as the *Soyuz* commander.[4] The crew lived on the ISS for four months. However, before they arrived, three space shuttle crews visited the ISS, stocking it with supplies and equipment.

Bullet-Proof Skin

Each of the ISS's living and research modules has to be lifted into orbit. To keep their weight low, they are made of aluminum. To protect the crew from micrometeoroids, these modules wear "bullet-proof vests," or micrometeoroid debris shields. These are made from layers of Kevlar, ceramic fabrics, and other materials, and surround each of the aluminum modules.

Robots and Sky Walkers

As parts of the ISS are placed in orbit, they must be attached to the station. Robotic arms do some of this work. The space shuttle's mechanical arm, and several ISS arms, operate as "space cranes" moving the parts into place. Space-walking astronauts do most of the assembly. They use special tools, wear pressurized suits, and use tethers to hook themselves to the ISS. Even though an astronaut wears a thruster backpack any time he or she is outside the station, walking in space is dangerous.[5] "When we do a spacewalk without the presence of a docked space shuttle, drifting away would be a fatal mistake," said ISS science officer Don Pettit.[6] Astronauts could also be hit by micrometeorites. This is why NASA built the Robonaut.

▶ Robonaut

Robonaut is a humanoid robot that will perform some work outside the ISS. Robonaut is about the size of an astronaut in a space suit. It has flexible arms and gloves, complete with five fingers. The gloves have sensors and act the way a human hand does.[7] Robonaut's hand can work with small tools such as tweezers and common handheld tools.[8] Its head has two color cameras for stereoscopic eyes.

Robonaut - Microsoft Internet Explorer

File   Edit   View   Favorites   Tools   Help

Address http://vesuvius.jsc.nasa.gov/er_er/html/robonaut/robonaut.html   Go   Links

Robonaut

SUBSYSTEMS
Hands
Arms
Head
Controls
Avionics
Telepresence
Vision
Body
Simulation
Robo-autonomy

TOOLS
Materials
Analysis Tools
Software
 Development
MIT Hand

VIDEOS

Robonaut

Robonaut is a humanoid robot designed by the Robot Systems Technology Branch at NASA's Johnson Space Center in a collaborative effort with DARPA. The Robonaut project seeks to develop and demonstrate a robotic system that can function as an EVA astronaut equivalent. Robonaut jumps generations ahead by eliminating the robotic scars (e.g., special robotic grapples and targets) and specialized robotic tools of traditional on-orbit robotics. However, it still keeps the human operator in the control loop through its telepresence control system. Robonaut is

Internet

▲ Robonaut is a robot that has some of the characteristics of human astronauts. Soon NASA will have a Robonaut aboard the space station to carry out some tasks that are dangerous for humans.

This means it can see in three dimensions. Its "skin" is a woven material similar to the space-suit fabric. The skin protects vulnerable areas against radiation and the extreme temperatures in space.[9]

Robonaut will be under the control of an astronaut inside the ISS. Wearing special gloves and a headset, the astronaut will have virtual reality eyes and hands. He or she will communicate with Robonaut using a remote camera and monitor. Since its head is too small, Robonaut has its "brain" in its chest area. It cannot think like humans, handle complex tasks, or replace the decision-making abilities of human astronauts. During spacewalks, astronauts devote about one third of their time to tasks such as installing foot restraints and laying out tools. These will be routine jobs for Robonaut.[10]

Solar Power

Electrical power is an important resource on the ISS. It allows the crew to live and work comfortably. Computers run almost everything on the ISS, and they use a lot of electricity. Solar energy from the sun is the only readily available source of energy for the ISS. The ISS converts this energy to electrical power using a process called photovoltaics.

More than a quarter million silicon solar cells, mounted on eight large solar arrays, gather the solar energy.[11] The solar cells convert sunlight into electricity in the same way solar cells power a handheld calculator. The solar panels rotate so they face the sun as the station orbits Earth. However, when the ISS is in Earth's shadow, batteries supply power for the station. During the sunlit part of the orbit, the batteries are recharged. When the station is completed, the solar arrays will be as large as two

▲ The solar arrays on the ISS are panels that trap solar energy from the sun and convert it to electricity. This powers the space station while Earth is not blocking it from the sun. When it is blocked, the ISS is powered by batteries.

football fields.[12] They will generate enough energy to power fifty-five houses.[13]

The concept of a space station is not new. Jonathan Swift wrote about the city of Laputa, in his book *Gulliver's Travels*, which was published in 1726. Swift's city moved between the earth and the sky by magnetism.

Chapter 3

THE FIRST SPACE STATIONS

The International Space Station is not the first space station. In 1971, the Soviet Union launched *Salyut 1*, to study the physical, biological, and psychological effects of weightlessness. The first crew, aboard a *Soyuz 10* rocket attempted to dock with *Salyut* twice, but the hatch would not open. The mission failed, and the crew returned home. The next crew docked successfully and lived on the station for twenty-four days.[1]

A tragic accident occurred during the crew's return. A valve on *Soyuz* accidentally opened when it separated from *Salyut*, moments before the *Soyuz* was going to descend. The valve would normally open as the spacecraft descended, equalizing the pressure inside and outside of the spacecraft. Having the valve open too early in space was fatal. When the rescue team located the spacecraft, the crew was dead.

In 1975, the *Apollo–Soyuz* mission was the first space flight conducted jointly by the United States and the Soviet Union. The two spacecraft docked and conducted experiments. The two countries were still bitter rivals at that time. Yet, they worked together in peace.

In 1982, the *Cosmos 1267* docked to *Salyut 6*. This was an important step in the development of the ISS. It proved that large vehicles could dock to a space station.

Salyut 7 was the last of the Soviet space stations before the *Mir* modular space station.[2] It remained in orbit for about nine years.

http://www.hq.nasa.gov/office/pao/History/alsj/astp/astp-s74-17843.jpg - Microsoft Internet Explorer

File Edit View Favorites Tools Help

Address http://www.hq.nasa.gov/office/pao/History/alsj/astp/astp-s74-17843.jpg   Go Links

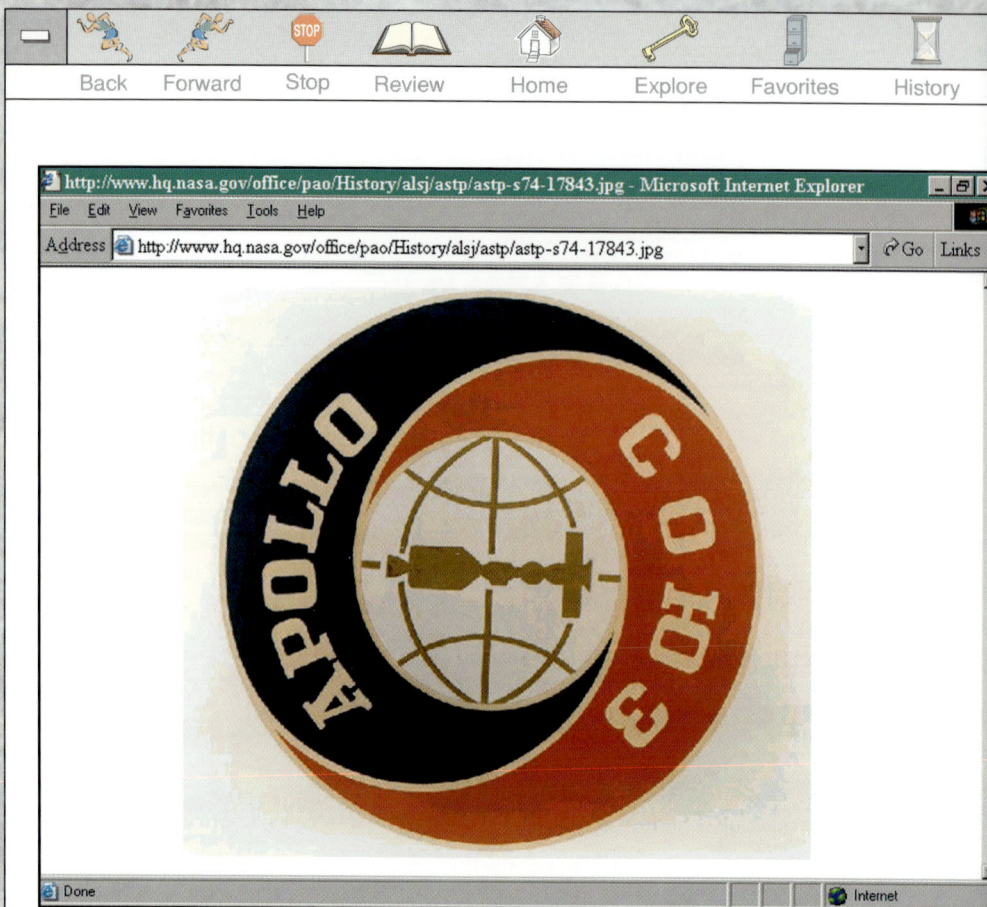

Done   Internet

▲ *This is the mission patch from the* Apollo-Soyuz *mission. Launched in 1975, this was the first mission in which the United States worked with the Soviet Union.*

▶ Skylab

The United States launched *Skylab*, its first manned space station, in 1973. It weighed nearly one hundred tons. *Skylab* was the converted third stage of a Saturn-V rocket and had two solar panels to supply power.

By now, scientists understood that exercise was important in space. *Skylab* had an exercise bike, and a docking port with air locks. This allowed the crew to make space-walks. Astronauts conducted more than three hundred experiments during the eight months they lived on board. Scientists learned about astronomy in ways that are impossible from Earth. Since *Skylab* orbited above Earth's atmosphere, there were no clouds or pollution to block the telescopes. *Skylab* proved that humans could live for long periods in space. The last crew returned to Earth in 1974, and five years later, the abandoned spacecraft burned up on reentry.

Russian Mir

Mir was launched in 1986. The first expansion module, Kvant, was added in 1987. With this addition, *Mir* became the world's first modular space station. It was

NOVA Online | Terror in Space | Take a Tour of Mir - Microsoft Internet Explorer

File Edit View Favorites Tools Help

Address http://www.pbs.org/wgbh/nova/mir/tour.html   Go   Links

PBS Home   Search   Programs A-Z   TV Schedules   Shop   Membership

(back to Terror in Space Home)

Take a Tour of *Mir*
Click on any module below to learn more about it and to see video of the interior.

Spektr
Space Shuttle Docking Module
Kristall
Priroda
Base Block
Kvant 2
Kvant 1

Internet

▲ *The Soviet Mir space station was launched in 1986. United States space shuttles began docking with Mir in 1995.*

▲ The Space Shuttle Atlantis docks with the Mir space station. Mir finally shut down in 1998, before burning up in the atmosphere in March 2001.

composed of different modules attached to docking ports. Together these modules made a larger station. *Mir* looked like a giant dragonfly with its wings outstretched.[3] Astronaut Jerry Linenger compared *Mir* to "six school buses all hooked together."[4] Other astronauts believe that *Mir* resembled a giant insect.

▶ Americans Dock with *Mir*

On June 29, 1995, America's space shuttles began docking with *Mir*. American and Russian scientists conducted experiments using *Mir* as a test bed for future space stations. Researchers performed tests that would help them build the ISS.[5] The space shuttle docked nine times with *Mir*, and astronauts from twelve different nations lived on *Mir* over the years.[6] Astronauts aboard *Mir* even grew the first crop of wheat in outer space.

Mir remained in orbit for fifteen years, three times longer than planned. As *Mir* grew older, it became more accident-prone. In February 1997, there was a fire on the station. There were computer malfunctions and power failures. In June 1997, a nearly fatal collision with the Russian supply rocket put a hole in the station, almost killing the crew.

In June 1998, *Mir* shut down. The empty spacecraft burned up on reentry in March 2001.[7] *Mir*'s end coincided with the first successful U.S.-Russian expedition to the ISS.

With the ISS in orbit, life became a little more comfortable for space station crew members. The ISS is larger than *Mir*, and scientists knew more about living in space.

Chapter 4

HOME SWEET SPACE STATION

Space is the most hostile environment for humans to live and work. It is cold, and there is no air to breathe or water to drink. However, living inside the International Space Station is almost like being on Earth. There is clean air, water, and food.

To maintain an orbit, the space station travels at 17,500 miles per hour (28,163.5 kilometers per hour),

http://spaceflight.nasa.gov/gallery/images/shuttle/sts-92/lores/s99-05103.jpg - Microsoft Internet Explorer

File   Edit   View   Favorites   Tools   Help

Address http://spaceflight.nasa.gov/gallery/images/shuttle/sts-92/lores/s99-05103.jpg   Go | Links

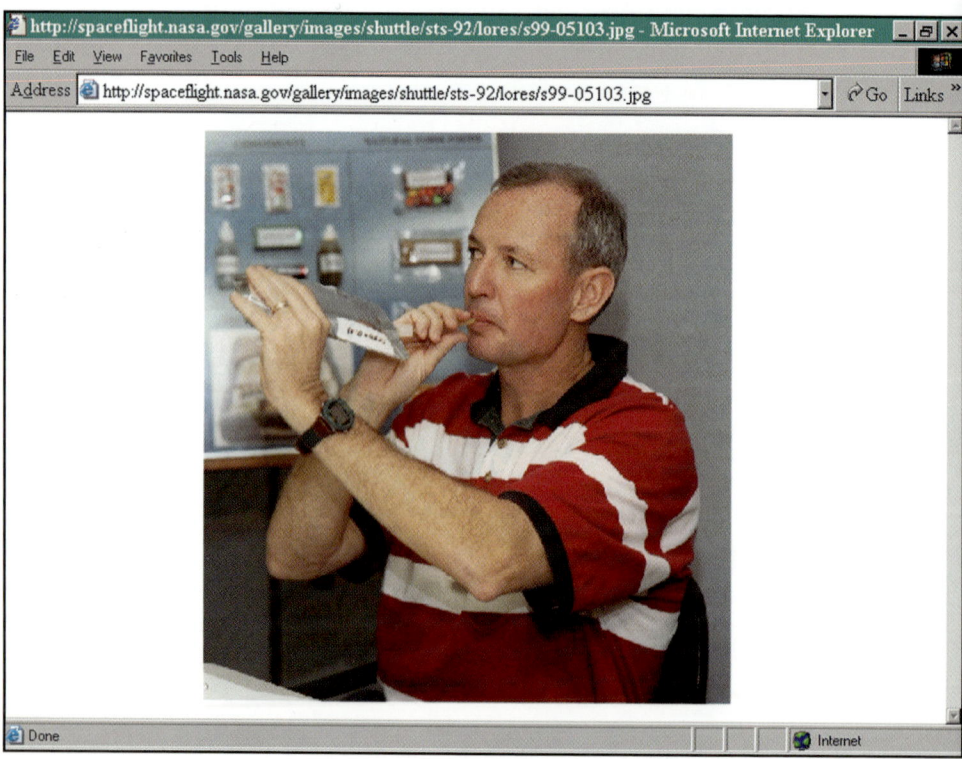

Done   Internet

▲ *In space there is certainly no running water. However, the astronauts make do with packaged drinks and food items.*

about five miles per second (8 kilometers per second). If you could bring the station down to 1,000 feet (305 meters) at this speed, it could travel from the west coast of the United States to the east coast in about nine minutes.[1]

▶ Microgravity

Gravity is what keeps our feet on the ground. Anytime we drop or throw something, we are watching gravity in action. On Earth, our feet are pulled to the ground by one "g" of gravity. We believe gravity causes plants to root into the ground and encourages fluids to mix. On the ISS, gravity is only a small fraction of that on Earth. This is called microgravity, or "zero-g." Sometimes it is called weightlessness. Microgravity describes this very weak gravitational effect.

Because of gravity, all artificial satellites like the ISS try to fall back to Earth. If a person on the ISS drops a pencil, it floats because the ISS, the person, and the pencil, are all in free fall toward Earth. Since there is this gravitational pull on the ISS, small engines on the ISS need to be used to reboost it to its proper orbit.

▶ Humans in Microgravity

In microgravity, a person's muscles and bones do not work as hard as they do on Earth. On the ISS, the crew must exercise or their muscles will atrophy, or weaken, and their bones will lose density. The only known way to reduce bone density loss is to place stress on the bones. Astronauts must exercise two hours every day. This may include running on a treadmill, riding a stationary bike, or using a "weightlifting" device that uses rubber bands instead of iron weights.[2] There are other health issues in

▲ *NBL stands for neutral buoyancy laboratory. This training facility allows astronauts to practice how they will have to move while they are in space.*

microgravity. Wounds heal more slowly, and the immune system weakens. Scientists do not yet know why.

▶ Artificial Gravity

In the 1950s, rocket pioneer Wernher von Braun envisioned a wheel-shaped space station that would spin like a carnival ride. The spinning would create a centrifugal force. That force would create artificial gravity. This idea was not practical at that time, but scientists adapted his idea to help today's astronauts.[3] Scientists are developing a small, human-powered centrifuge. An astronaut pedals a bike around a 360-degree circle. Depending on the speed the astronaut is going and the size of track, he or she will experience some artificial gravity.[4] This may help prevent bone density loss.

Return to Earth

Gravity pulls blood and fluids toward the lower body and feet. In microgravity, the fluids move to the upper body, neck, and head. It can cause some astronauts to get puffy faces. There are receptors in the carotid arteries in the neck that sense this extra fluid. The body's natural response is to eliminate this fluid. On reentry, gravity pulls the fluids back down to the astronaut's feet, leaving less in the brain. The body has eliminated what it sensed to be excess fluid. As a result, the astronauts must drink a combination of water and salt tablets, a hypotonic solution like a sports drink, or they will get dizzy or black out.[5]

The Neutral Buoyancy Laboratory

Part of an astronaut's training is to learn how to move safely in microgravity. The 6.2-million-gallon neutral buoyancy laboratory (NBL) is four stories deep. It allows astronauts to safely practice the movements they will use during a spacewalk. The large tank contains a mock-up of the shuttle's payload bay. Astronauts simulate setting up antennas and testing the use of foot restraints and hand-holds. They wear an underwater version of a space suit and are made neutrally buoyant by attaching floats and weights to their suits, until they neither rise nor fall in the tank.[6] For every hour the astronaut expects to walk in space, he or she will practice for about ten hours in the NBL.[7]

Conserving Water and Oxygen in Space

Since water is in short supply on the ISS, almost every drop is recycled. Each crew member is allowed only about forty-three ounces of water—a little more than a quart—per day.[8] The crews do not take showers, because the floating water bubbles would bounce around. Instead, they take sponge baths. They wash their hair with dry shampoo and wipe it off with a damp towel. The water recycling system reclaims water from the hydrogen fuel cells, toothbrushing, hand washing, the crew's breath, and even from the toilet. Laboratory animals even have their breath and urine recycled.[9] The air-conditioning system condenses the moisture from the air and purifies it. Without careful recycling, 5,000 gallons of water would have to be resupplied from Earth each year.[10]

The oxygen people breathe on Earth comes from green plants, algae, and phytoplankton, through a process called photosynthesis. When plants are exposed to light, they convert carbon dioxide and water into glucose and oxygen. Although there are green plants for experiments on the ISS, there are not enough to make breathable air. Most of the station's oxygen comes from a process called "electrolysis." This process uses electricity from the solar panels to split water molecules into hydrogen and oxygen gases. Astronauts breathe the oxygen, and the hydrogen is vented into space.[11]

▶ Personal Satellite Assistant

There are many tasks for the crew aboard the ISS. They must monitor the amount of oxygen, carbon dioxide, and other gases in the air. They will even measure bacterial growth, air temperature, and air pressure.

Scientists decided that a small mobile robot could perform these tasks. The Personal Satellite Assistant (PSA) is a small intelligent robot that will serve as another set of eyes, ears, and nose for the crew.[12] About the size of a softball, the PSA will have sensors to monitor the environment. It will have a camera for video conferencing, navigation sensors,

http://ic.arc.nasa.gov/projects/psa/psadesription.gif - Microsoft Internet Explorer

File   Edit   View   Favorites   Tools   Help

Address   http://ic.arc.nasa.gov/projects/psa/psadesription.gif   Go   Links

Done   Internet

▲ *PSAs, or Personal Satellite Assistants, are small robots that will help future astronauts measure things such as air pressure, temperature, and the amount of bacteria that may be growing aboard the ISS.*

and wireless network connections. It will even move under its own power, so it can zip around the spacecraft.[13]

▶ Eating and Sleeping in Space

Astronauts use sleeping bags to restrain themselves while they sleep so they do not float around. On the ISS, there are two small crew cabins. Each is large enough for just one person. Inside each crew cabin is a sleeping bag and a large window to look out into space. The crew uses sleep masks when they sleep. Otherwise, they would see the sun rise and set every ninety minutes. The sunlight entering the window is enough to disturb a sleeper who is not wearing a sleep mask. They also use earplugs to block out noises from fans, pumps, and equipment.

Sometimes, the ISS has three crew members living together. The third person, if it is okay with the commander, can sleep anywhere in the ISS, as long as he attaches him or herself to something.

Even though engineers have tried to make the environment on board the ISS as close to Earth as possible, the crew has major adjustments to make. The ISS has personal hygiene stations where the crew can wash and use the toilet. The toilets are similar to those in an airliner, except they have foot restraints and seat belts. Instead of the bio-wastes being flushed away with water, they are swept away with a suction system. These wastes are not

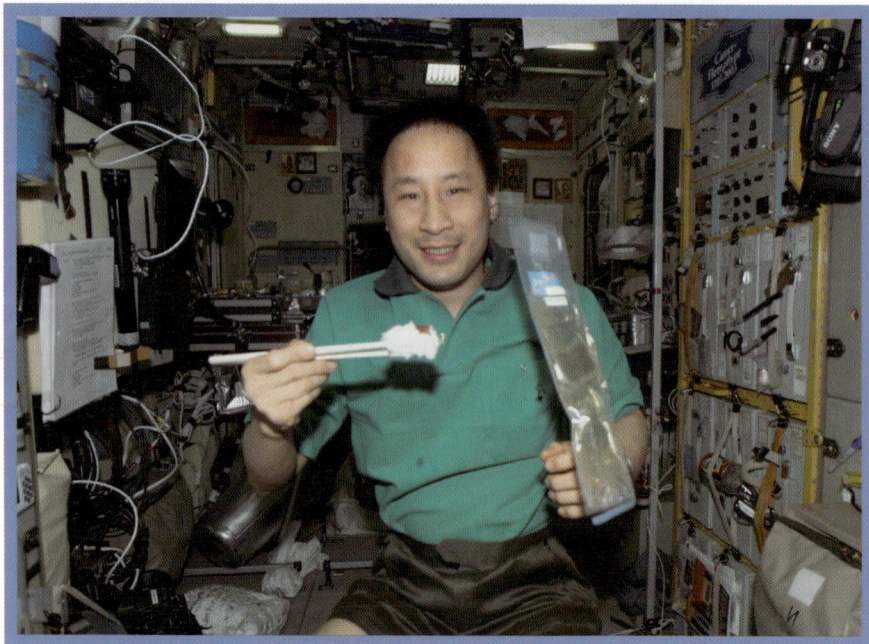

▲ *The quality of food aboard the ISS and other space flights has improved quite a bit since the early days of space travel. Astronaut Edward T. Lu is using chopsticks to eat his meal.*

dumped overboard. They are dried and stored and taken back to Earth on the shuttle.

The early *Mercury* and *Gemini* astronauts had to eat bite-sized food-cubes covered with gelatin, to prevent crumbs. In microgravity, crumbs are dangerous because they float and can get into the equipment. The food is much better now. Along with a refrigerator, the crew has a microwave oven, and they eat shrimp cocktail, steak, and chicken salsa.[14]

The ISS gets all its food from the space shuttle or Russia's *Progress* cargo spacecraft. Some of the food is dried, and water is added to it at mealtime. Most of the food is packed in pouches and ready to eat, either cold or heated. Fresh fruit, veggies, milk, and ice cream are shipped up to the ISS on the space shuttles and *Progress* cargo spacecraft.

▶ Taking Out the Trash

Since there are no clothes washers or dryers on board the ISS, the crews dress in "disposable" clothing. When the clothing is dirty, they throw it away. Trash, such as food packages, human waste, and solid waste from science projects, is not easy to recycle. Still, someone has to take out the trash. The shuttle and *Progress* do this job. Every shuttle that brings up fresh supplies turns into a trash truck. When it leaves, it takes many sealed trash bags back to Earth. Since the Russian *Progress* craft does not carry a crew, it gets rid of trash in a more exciting way. After its cargo is unloaded, the trash bags are loaded aboard. Then *Progress* is shut tight and it heads back to Earth. As it reenters Earth's atmosphere, it heats up and catches fire. Both the spacecraft and all the trash burn up in the atmosphere.

Wiping Out Germs

Microbes were the first things to live on the ISS. They came from Earth, carried on parts of the ISS and by the crews who assembled the ISS. These tiny microbes are viruses, bacteria, and fungi. These "bugs" now live on the surfaces of the ISS, on the systems, and in the astronauts' bodies. Scientists have found that microbes grow rapidly in microgravity. If not controlled, they could make the crew sick. The crews' own bodies keep most of the germs under control. Other microbes are removed by the station's air and water cleaning systems. Still, the astronauts have to fight the microbes that could cause harm. Their daily duties include wiping surfaces in their work and living areas with cloths that have a germ-killing liquid on them.

Radiation in Space

Earth's atmosphere filters out most of the dangerous radiation from space. However, when astronauts travel outside the atmosphere, they are exposed to this radiation. Scientists have developed some protection against this radiation. It is found in hydrogen compounds. One material that is lightweight and contains hydrogen is polyethylene. A three-inch shield of polyethylene will block about 35 percent of the radiation throughout the interior of the station. Astronauts also take large doses of vitamins A and C to help absorb the radiation-produced particles in their bodies.[15]

Lifeboat in Space

Like a ship at sea, the ISS needs a lifeboat. If the crew has to abandon the ISS, a crew return vehicle is needed. Currently, a Russian *Soyuz* spacecraft that can carry three crew members, is docked to ISS to serve as a lifeboat. Later,

▲ *Crew Return Vehicles (CRVs) are docked at the ISS at all times in case of emergency. A CRV serves as the crew's lifeboat.*

the X–38 Crew Return Vehicle (CRV), will serve as the lifeboat. It will be able to return up to seven crew members to Earth. In an emergency, the CRV would undock and return to Earth much like a space shuttle. A steerable parafoil parachute will open at an altitude of about forty thousand feet. Because it has skids instead of wheels, it can glide to a landing almost anywhere on land and does not need a runway.

The ISS will serve as a long-term research platform to help us learn ways to improve and preserve life on Earth. On the ISS, scientists will perform experiments not possible on Earth.

Chapter 5

RESEARCH ON THE INTERNATIONAL SPACE STATION

The International Space Station is useful for growing and experimenting with proteins, enzymes, bacteria, and viruses. In microgravity, bacteria and cancer cells grow larger and looser shapes. Scientists can study their growth more easily and perhaps get a better understanding of the basic building blocks of life.[1] The knowledge from these experiments may help doctors develop new drugs. Cultures grown in the ISS may be used to test new treatments for cancer without risking harm to the patients.[2] The ongoing research might lead to cures for diabetes and

▲ One drawback about space travel is its effects on the human body. Astronaut David Wolf spent over 143 days in space, and the effects of space have caused some damage to his pelvic (hip) bone.

In October 1989, the Galileo ▶ Probe was sent to gather information about Jupiter and various asteroids.

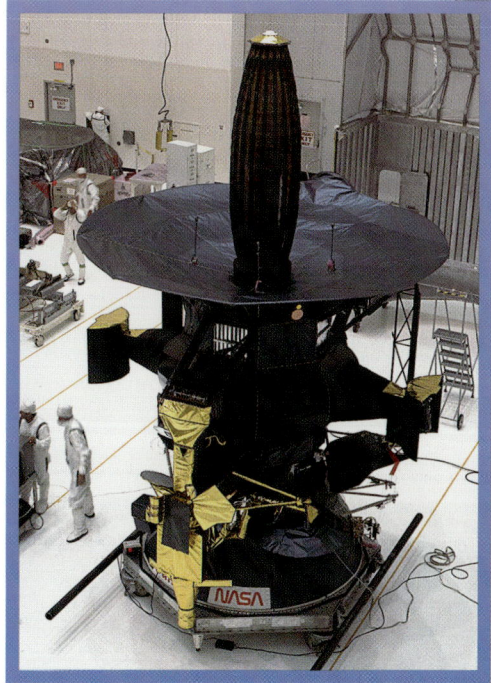

other serious illnesses. The search may also lead to a way to grow human tissues and possibly create new organs .[3]

In space, the body loses calcium, a mineral necessary for strong bones, at a rate of nearly one percent a month. Without gravity to put a load on the skeleton, air molecules in bones expand. This decreases the bone's density, and the bones dissolve away. Astronaut David Wolf, who flew two shuttle missions, spent more than 143 days in space. He lost about 13 percent of the bone mineral in his pelvis.[4] Scientists are searching for ways to prevent this.

In twenty or thirty years, we may send people to Mars or beyond. In October 1989, NASA launched the unmanned *Galileo* spacecraft to Jupiter, the next planet beyond Mars. It arrived over five years later.[5] Before humans can make such a trip, we must learn how very long periods of microgravity affect the body. Astronauts are using the ISS for these studies.

Scientists are growing zeolite crystals on the ISS. Among other useful things, these crystals absorb hydrogen. Scientists hope one day to replace gasoline-burning cars with hydrogen-burning cars. These zeolite crystals may one day be used to line the fuel tank, in place of gasoline. The hydrogen stored in the crystals would power the car.[6]

▷ Earth Science

The ISS will allow us to study Earth's climate from outside the atmosphere. Scientists will study large-scale, long-term changes in the environment. They will be able to forecast weather more accurately, and provide early warning of hurricanes and other violent storms. They will also be able to study the effects of air pollution, such as smog over cities, water pollution, and oil spills. From the ISS, they will have a worldwide view not available on the ground.

Some experiments will take place outside the ISS, in outer space. These will study long-term exposure to radiation, micrometeoroids, and the extreme temperatures

▲ Scientists will be able to study Earth's weather patterns from the ISS. Hurricane Isabel struck the Eastern United States in the summer of 2003. This image of the eye of the storm was taken from the ISS.

▲ *Being in microgravity allows scientists to do experiments not possible on Earth. In this image, astronauts (from left to right) Robert L. Curbeam, Mark L. Polansky, Kenneth D. Cockrell, Thomas D. Jones, and Marsha S. Ivins take a break from working on a laboratory aboard the ISS.*

of space. These studies may lead to better planning for long-distance space travel.

Flames burn differently in microgravity. In the absence of convection currents, in which warm air rises and cool air sinks, scientists can study the combustion process in ways not possible on Earth. The absence of convection will allow scientists to study molten metals more thoroughly than on Earth. From these studies, scientists hope to create better metal alloys (substances made from two or more metals).

Someday, the ISS may be used as a base camp for future trips to the moon and the universe. It may also act as a dock for future spacecraft.

Chapter 6

BASE CAMP TO THE UNIVERSE

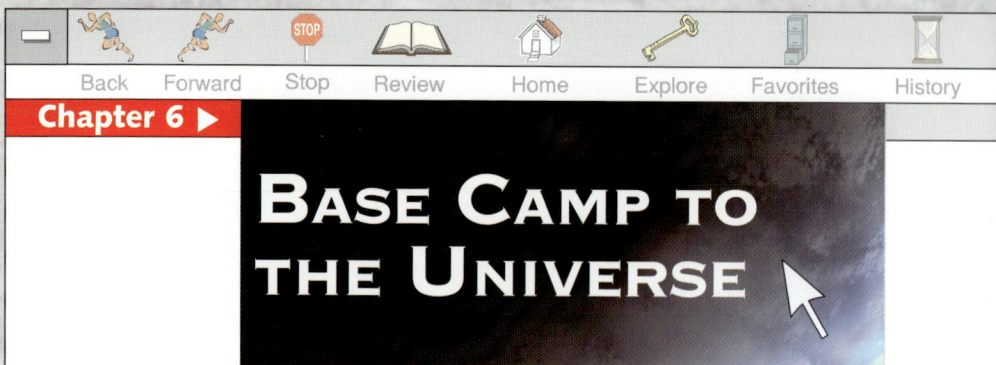

One day in the future, a space shuttle will dock with the International Space Station. The astronauts will transfer to a new type of spacecraft docked at the ISS that will explore the depths of space. The future spacecraft will need to be lightweight and propelled by a reliable source of energy. The strange spacecraft may look like a giant kite that travels

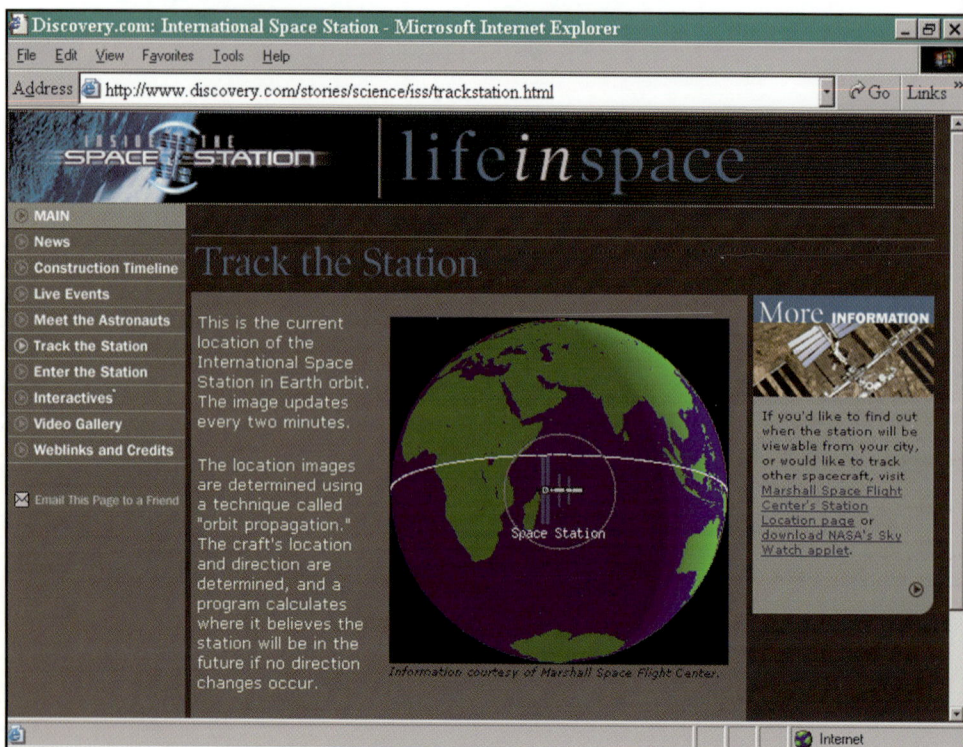

Discovery.com: International Space Station - Microsoft Internet Explorer

File Edit View Favorites Tools Help

Address http://www.discovery.com/stories/science/iss/trackstation.html Go Links

SPACE STATION life*in*space

MAIN
News
Construction Timeline
Live Events
Meet the Astronauts
Track the Station
Enter the Station
Interactives
Video Gallery
Weblinks and Credits

Email This Page to a Friend

Track the Station

This is the current location of the International Space Station in Earth orbit. The image updates every two minutes.

The location images are determined using a technique called "orbit propagation." The craft's location and direction are determined, and a program calculates where it believes the station will be in the future if no direction changes occur.

Space Station

Information courtesy of Marshall Space Flight Center.

More **INFORMATION**

If you'd like to find out when the station will be viewable from your city, or would like to track other spacecraft, visit Marshall Space Flight Center's Station Location page or download NASA's Sky Watch applet.

▲ *The International Space Station orbits Earth from about 240 miles (386 kilometers) away. The Marshall Space Flight Center tracks where the ISS is at all times.*

on solar winds from the sun. The sails will be driven by photons—particles of energy emitted from sunlight.[1]

The ISS gives us endless visions and possibilities for exploring Earth's resources and the solar system. Humans may use it as a platform to launch future space colonies. One day it may be a space tourist stop. The ISS may act as a shipyard in space, where the vehicles that will explore deep space will be built. Someday people may use it as a base camp to mine asteroids for precious and rare metals. By exploring space, scientists hope to discover how life began. At 10 million miles per hour, about 250 times faster than our fastest spacecraft travels, a trip to the nearest star system would take three hundred years.[2] The ISS may serve as the base camp to explore the universe.

▶ Columbia Disaster

On February 1, 2003, space shuttle *Columbia* broke up on reentry, killing all seven crew members on board. Mental-health counselors on the ground helped the three-member crew aboard the ISS deal with their grief following the disaster. The crew said their emotions over the loss of their seven friends on *Columbia* seemed to be greater in orbit, because they were isolated and so far away.[3]

NASA stopped all space shuttle flights until the cause of the accident was known. This had a serious impact on building the ISS. The crew was supposed to switch in March, on the shuttle *Atlantis*. With all shuttles grounded, a new plan was developed. The Russian *Progress* M–47 cargo craft would resupply the ISS with food and water until the shuttles are flying again. The three-man crew returned to Earth in June. NASA will keep a two-person crew rotating every six months on the ISS.[4] These crews

▲ *This is a full view of the International Space Station as it appeared on December 2, 2002.*

will launch aboard a Russian *Soyuz* TMA–2 spacecraft until the shuttles return to flight.[5]

The astronauts who live on the ISS know there are risks from micrometeorites, and radiation from the sun. Still, they feel the risks are worth it. Astronaut Andy Allen said, "I know spaceflight is a risk, and I know I may not come back from a flight . . . the risk of losing your life is outweighed by what space exploration is going to bring, maybe not directly to your family, but to the world."[6]

The creative forces behind the possibilities of space exploration are the people—those who see beyond what is currently possible. We do not know what might be found out there, and the ISS will be used to discover the unknown. It will very likely be the greatest adventure of the twenty-first century.

Chapter Notes

Chapter 1. Danger in Space

1. Maia Weinstock, "Orbiting Junk Continues to Threaten International Space Station," *Space.com*, September 5, 2000, <http://www.space.com./scienceastronomy/planetearth/space_junk_000901.html> (October 24, 2003).

2. Robert Roy Britt, "Space Junk: The Stuff Left Behind," *Space.com*, October 19, 2000, <http://www.space.com/spacewatch/space_junk.html> (October 24, 2003).

3. Ibid.

4. Robert Coontz Jr., "Space Junk," *Astronomy*, December 2000, vol. 28, issue 12, p. 56.

5. Britt, "Space Junk."

6. Maia Weinstock, "Orbiting Junk Continues to Threaten International Space Station."

7. Britt, "Space Junk."

Chapter 2. Building the International Space Station

1. NASA, "International Space Station Assembly," NASA document LG-1999-09-522-HQ.

2. Mary F. Bell, "International Space Station: Turning Science Fiction Into Science Fact," NASA Facts, May 9, 2000, <http://www.hq.nasa.gov/office/pao/facts/HTML/FS-004-HQ.html> (October 24, 2003).

3. Kylie Moritz, "Endeavour Delivers Unity Node to International Space Station," STS-88, June 13, 2003, <http://spaceflight.nasa.gov/shuttle/archives/sts-88/index.html> (October 24, 2003).

4. Bill Shepherd, "Preflight Interview," *Human Spaceflight*, May 16, 2002, <http://spaceflight.nasa.gov/station/crew/exp1/intshepherd.html> (October 24, 2003).

5. Jason Quinn, NASA, e-mail to author, dated March 27, 2003.

6. Don Pettit, "Getting Ready for a Space Walk," *Space Station Science*, January 15, 2003, <http://science.nasa.gov/ppod/y2003/08apr spacewalk.htm> (October 24, 2003).

7. *Inside the Space Station*, Discovery Channel Video, Discovery Channel Films, LLC., 2000.

8. Chris Culbert, "Robonaut *Video Transcripts*," Video Transcripts, March 19, 2001, <http://vesuvius.jsc.nasa.gov/er_er/html/robonaut/transcripts.htm#hand_motion> (October 24, 2003).

9. Richard Stenger, "'Robonaut' prepares for Spacewalking Duties," June 13, 2000, <http://cgi.cnn.com/2000/TECH/space/06/13/robonaut/index.html> (October 24, 2003).

10. Ibid.

11. Glenn Research Center, "Powering the Future," NASA Facts FS-2000-11-006-GRC.

12. *Inside the Space Station*, Discovery Channel Video, Discovery Channel Films, LLC., 2000.

13. Glenn Research Center, "Powering the Future."

Chapter 3. The First Space Stations

1. NASA, "International Space Station Assembly," NASA document LG-1999-09-522-HQ.

2. Sarah M. Murphy, "Salyut 7 Space Station, Crews," *The Astronaut Connection*, February 8, 2000, <http://www.nauts.com/vehicles/80s/salyut7/index.html> (April 3, 2003).

3. Kylie Moritz, "Shuttle-Mir Background: Descriptions of Mir," *History*, September 17, 2003, <http://spaceflight.nasa.gov/history/shuttle-mir/history/to-h-b-descriptions.htm> (October 24, 2003).

4. Kylie Moritz, "Mir's 15 Years," *Mir Space Station*, October 3, 2003, <http://spaceflight.nasa.gov/history/shuttle-mir/spacecraft/s-mir-15yrs-main.htm> (October 24, 2003).

5. John Uri, "ISS Risk Mitigation," *Shuttle-Mir History*, July 16, 1999, <http://spaceflight.nasa.gov/history/shuttle-mir/science/sc-iss.htm> (October 24, 2003).

6. NASA, "International Space Station Assembly," NASA document LG-1999-09-522-HQ.

7. Moritz, "Mir's 15 Years."

Chapter 4. Home Sweet Space Station

1. Jeff Hanley, "Mission Control Answers Your Questions," *NASA Human Spaceflight*, January 22, 2003, <http://spaceflight.nasa.gov/feedback/expert/answer/MCC/01_14_16_53_18.html> (October 24, 2003).

2. Ed Lu, "Ed Lu's Answers," *ISS Crew Answers: Expedition 7*, September 24, 2003, <http://spaceflight.nasa.gov/feedback/expert/answer/isscrew/index.html> (October 24, 2003).

3. Patrick Barry, "Wheels in the Sky," *Wheels in the Sky*, May 26, 2000, <http://science.nasa.gov/headlines/y2000/ast26may_1m.htm> (October 24, 2003).

4. Karen Miller, "Space Medicine," *Science@NASA*, September 30, 2002, <http://science.nasa.gov/headlines/y2002/30sept_spacemedicine.htm> (October 24, 2003).

5. John Curry, "Mission Control Answers Your Questions," *Human Spaceflight*, October 13, 2002, <http://spaceflight.nasa.gov/feedback/expert/answer/MCC/sts-112/09_12_09_40_34.html> (October 24, 2003).

6. Kylie Moritz, "Living in Space," *Human Spaceflight*, April 18, 2003, <http://spaceflight.nasa.gov/living/index.html> (October 24, 2003).

7. *Inside the Space Station*, Discovery Channel Video, Discovery Channel Films, LLC., 2000.

8. Jason Quinn, NASA, e-mail to author, dated March 27, 2003.

9. Patrick L. Barry and Tony Phillip, "Water on the Space Station: Making a Splash in Space," *Human Spaceflight*, April 18, 2003, <http://spaceflight.nasa.gov/living/factsheets/water2.html> (October 24, 2003).

10. Ibid.

11. Don Pettit, "Don Pettit's Answers*,*" *ISS Crew Answers: Expedition Six*, May 1, 2003, <http://spaceflight.nasa.gov/feedback/expert/answer/isscrew/pettit2.html> (October 24, 2003).

12. Michael Mewhinney, "NASA Developing Autonomous Robot For Future Space Missions," *NASA Ames Research Center*, September 8, 1999, <http://amesnews.arc.nasa.gov/releases/1999/99_53AR.html> (April 3, 2003).

13. Jeff Jones, "Personal Satellite Assistant," *NASA Ames Research Center*, n.d., <http://ic.arc.nasa.gov/projects/psa/> (October 24, 2003).

14. Moritz, "Living in Space."

15. Rosemary Wilson, "Cures for Space Travelers," *New Science*, March 3, 2003, <http://liftoff.msfc.nasa.gov/news/2003/news-medicine.asp> (October 24, 2003).

Chapter 5. Research on the International Space Station

1. William R. Newcott, "Space Exploration: A Good Investment?" *National Geographic*, June 1999, <http://www.nationalgeographic.com/ngm/9906/forum/space-essay.html> (October 24, 2003).

2. NASA, "Research on the International Space Station," NASA document LG-1999-06-455-HQ.

3. *Inside the Space Station*, Discovery Channel Video, Discovery Channel Films, LLC. 2000.

4. Ibid.

5. Phil Davis, "Galileo," *Missions to Jupiter*, October 28, 2002, <http://solarsystem.nasa.gov/missions/jup_missns/jup-galileo.html> (October 24, 2003).

6. Dr. Tony Phillips and Steve Price, "Rocks in Your Gas Tank," *Science@NASA*, <http://science.nasa.gov/headlines/y2003/17apr_zeolite.htm?list893828> (October 24, 2003).

Chapter 6. Base Camp to the Universe

1. Dr. David P. Stern, "Gradual Acceleration by Low Thrust," *Far-out Pathways to Space: Solar Sails*, December 13, 2001, <http://www-spof.gsfc.nasa.gov/stargaze/Solsail.htm> (October 24, 2003).

2. Joel Achenbach, "Life Beyond Earth," *National Geographic*, January 2000, p. 26.

3. Mike Schneider, "Psychologists Help Crew on International Space Station," *SpaceFlight*, February 21, 2003, <http://www.space.com/missionlaunches/iss_counsel_030221.html> (October 24, 2003).

4. Frank Morring, Jr., et. al. "ISS: A New Crew of Two," *Aviation Week & Space Technology*, March 3, 2003, p. 24.

5. CBS News Coverage of Shuttle Mission STS–107, February 27, 2003.

6. Tony Reich, ed., *Space Shuttle—The First Twenty Years* (New York: DK Publishing, Inc., 2002), p. 274.

Further Reading

Bond, Peter. *Guide to Space*. New York: Dorling Kindersley, Inc., 1999.

Branley, Franklyn M. *The International Space Station*. Illustrated by True Kelley. New York: HarperCollins, 2000.

Campbell, Ann-Jeanette. *Amazing Space: A Book of Answers for Kids*. New York: John Wiley & Sons, Inc., 1997.

Caprara, Giovanni. *Living In Space: From Science Fiction to the International Space Station*. Buffalo, N.Y.: Firelfly Books, 2000.

Cole, Michael D. Astronauts *Training for Space*. Springfield, N.J.: Enslow Publishers, 1999.

———. *International Space Station: A Space Mission*. Berkeley Heights, N.J.: Enslow Publishers, Inc., 1999.

———. *NASA Space Vehicles: Capsules, Shuttles, and Space Stations*. Berkeley Heights, N.J.: Enslow Publishers, Inc., 2000.

Dyson, Marianne. *Space Station Science: Life in Free Fall*. New York: Scholastic, 1999.

Stott, Carole. *Space Exploration*. New York: Alfred A. Knopf, 1997.

Trotman, Felicity. *Living In Space*. Hauppauge, N.Y.: Barron's Educational Series, 2000.